Eastern European Poets Series #43

Artis Ostups

GESTURES

Translated from the Latvian
by Jayde Will

Gestures
© Artis Ostups, 2018
English Translation © Jayde Will, 2018
Introduction © Kārlis Vērdiņš, 2018

Originally published 2016 in Latvian as *Žesti* by Neputns (Riga, Latvia)

ISBN 978-1-937027-90-2

First Edition, First Printing, 2018
1000 copies

Eastern European Poets Series #43

Ugly Duckling Presse
The Old American Can Factory
232 Third Street #E-303
Brooklyn, New York 11215

Distributed to the trade by SPD/Small Press Distribution (USA), Raincoast Books via Coach House Books (Canada), Inpress (UK)

Typeset by Katherine Bogden
Design by Katherine Bogden and *Don't Look Now!*
Typeset in Adobe Caslon Pro & Trivia Humanist
Interiors printed offset and bound by Thomson-Shore
Covers printed offset at Prestige Printing on French paper

This book is made possible by generous support from the Latvian Writers Union (Latvijas Rakstnieku Savienība), Ministry of Culture of the Republic of Latvia, and LATVIA 100. Additional support was provided by the National Endowment for the Arts and by the New York State Council on the Arts.

Kultūras ministrija

Latvijas Rakstnieku savienība

ART WORKS.

National Endowment for the Arts
arts.gov

Latvija 100

NEW YORK STATE OF OPPORTUNITY. | Council on the Arts

REACHING OUT

Artis Ostups' third collection of poetry, *Žesti* (*Gestures*), is one of the very few Latvian poetry books I have in my small apartment with a single, crammed bookshelf in St. Louis. Sometimes, when it is already dark, I take it with me in my bed to flip through its pages and read one or two poems just to refresh myself after reading on world-systems analysis and Planetary Modernism. This book has become for me a symbol of Latvian contemporary poetry as I know it and love it.

Every new generation of Latvian poets has tried to avoid the claustrophobic existence of "small literature." This is a life that happens in a rather small and predictable poetic scene where everybody knows everybody else and where everybody always feels slightly frustrated by the vague feeling of things happening too slowly, too narrowly, too repeating. Whenever you attempt to be a flâneur who loses himself in an evening crowd, you will meet an acquaintance and you'll end up sitting at the same bar talking about your other acquaintances.

Ostups embodies for me the kind of poet who is simultaneously one of us and a stranger. Although born and bred in the Latvian poetic scene, he is constantly looking beyond its comfort zones and learning from the outside what he cannot learn from the Latvian tradition of poetry, which is itself usually defined as a chain of belated reactions to international modernism. Ostups acknowledges Rimbaud's *Illuminations* as one of his sources of inspiration, however, it is impossible to miss many other influences.

The spirit of the poems in *Gestures* seems to dwell somewhere in the period of *La Belle Époque*, drawing its energy from the capitals of the Austro-Hungarian, German, and Russian Empires, giving us imagined glimpses of their material culture, everyday habits, and mood in the streets as well as the particular etiquette of human relations. And just next to that, there is the first half of the 20th century, with its modernist and avant-garde art practices and social reforms. What unites both of these eras in Ostups' poems is their suppressed emotionality and fragmentary nature: we see a world we are somehow longing for; at the same time it remains always alien. The principle of defamiliarization, formulated by Russian formalist Viktor Shklovsky in 1917, is here both a poetic strategy and a gesture itself that speaks to the circumstance of its necessity.

Ostups belongs to the new generation of Latvian poets who are passionately interested in modernist poetry. Their utopian project might be described as creating modernist Latvian poetry that would be both contemporary and past-impregnated – as if they were nostalgic about some trends in Latvian literary modernism that never came to be one hundred years ago. As if there was something deeply wrong with Latvian poetry without acting on these trends. As if there were a painful necessity to overcome both the contemporary nationalist stereotypes of Latvian public discourse and the limitations of Soviet occupation, when modernism was wildly combated by the authorities.

This book makes me sure that this vision is not impossible. I believe in the world created in the long poem "Three Photographs," one of Ostups' most striking works. I see Franz Kafka, Walter Benjamin, and Artis Ostups all meeting as children. Artis would let Walter hug his little monkey while

Franz would put his big Spanish hat on Artis' head. I see these gestures transcending time and space, if only for a moment. And I can return to my World-systems analysis, and read about the core, the semi-peripheral and the peripheral literatures, the latter's endless dependency on what came before.

Kārlis Vērdiņš
St. Louis, 2018

GESTURES

AFTER REGAINING INDEPENDENCE

When we left the church, stars gathered around the moon's crumbled horn above the red cornice of the post office, seen through greasy glasses. My mother wore a black felt coat – winter pulled chalk across it like a schoolboy on a blackboard. Later I drew gates on my bedroom wall, while the plaster bust of a woman observed me from the top of the closet. Did the far-off clicks – from the railway and the highway – give hope for a different, more vast landscape? The gardens burned with a cawing, raven-black flame.

GESTURES

A fallen glove points to narrow tables abandoned in the sudden rain – they stand in a semi-circle around the small Italian restaurant, waiters darting about in the windows. As far as the gray glass allows one to surmise, their shirts are white as snow, though they have lost their envelope stiffness. One could only guess how the art of a glove, this orphan who has lost the tender hand of a woman, will be influenced by the blind and hurried footsteps of the evening. Not far away, swinging up to the roof, bare branches become fingers trembling in hatred, as if preparing to strangle someone. This, it seems, is jealousy for the tower's crown – a nest for long shadows, which on sunny days describe a buzzing street and attract the glance of a flâneur. Like a pleasant change – the bird's coat of arms on the reverse of the branch bundle with wings stretched out in a drenched greeting.

AN INLAND LIGHTHOUSE

Poland at night – a black, taciturn landscape, as if it were photographed with the lid still on. Emptiness after emptiness. Pulsating here and there: "HOTEL FOX, DRIVE-IN." The light, reflecting in the dark screen, is an inland lighthouse for weary truckers. A bus sways on the bends of the narrow road and awakens me to an already-read book. Anonymous villages on the other side of the hills, on which the golden age of industry slumbers. Images from the past unite in fine facets like in an insect's eye. An insomnia machine with windows clouded by drunks has thrust me toward Europe's lowest point.

A SERVANT'S CONCERNS

A tapestry ails from the dim light of the kerosene lamp: rosy dark is the softly-slanted path of the hunters. "Like Diana on that prickly slope, some foggy illness is racing through my master," the good-natured servant speculates, setting about his work. The cotton wads are first moistened in spirit, then lit, and for a moment put in a cupping glass like a small lantern. "It can't be heart asthma," he calms himself groundlessly and puts the lamps on his pale back, which stick to it like the snouts of forest animals. The aristocrat wheezes heavily, as he is covered by a golden-colored blanket that darkens to rose. "I see my master," glancing back at the tapestry, the servant lingers in the doorway, "chirping in the treetops," and almost echoes a chirp, "with the princes on a hunt: dogs scurry in the underbrush, the sun blazes on the hilltop, demise glistens on the bayonet and in the might of my master."

AFTER RILKE

– everything will remain partially unsaid, but once someone wrote – my chest is like a lamp, lit up by a look, and it truly did shine for the pleasure of cicadas, as I inhaled the nightly scents of the mountains. Now the cracked screen, snowy like after a heavy blow, shows a raven stuck in oil and a lyre with frayed nerves – a marked-up sheet of paper, tossed in the grass, and me myself like paper as well – burned halfway, but my eyes will stay silent. What once was music and light, tones and cascades, is now a faint whisper and the lighter flame – look, it's going out in the last muse's face – before she comes and cuts –

SONNET

It was on the words of other poets, mostly dead ones, that he lingered, for hours spinning his own sonnets, fourths and long, finely branched-out sentences. One night he reached the pinnacle of a new cycle – a final third, the loftiness of which was supposed to counterbalance the neglected everyday. Still, it lacked powerful, poetic words: "heart" dried up, it was enveloped by "darkness," "fate" seemed silly, but "death" terrified one even more than "God" does in Baptist prayers. By chance he looked in the mirror where he found "reflection," "full moon".

MONSTROSITIES

What will remain of the market stalls, where brown coins lay down on red velvet, where stuffed animals break from their hooks and surrender themselves to expectant falls? Like blood smeared by a palm, your features blur – your dumpy countess-like face, which I abhor, blows away like sand from glass – and trivial loves, clothed for nightly walks, and accidental glances calm in that gold, which was not fated to wash me ashore next to you. Everything mocks you with a thousand tongues, sweet words collapse into prattle, and, as if pulled by the arm, life vanishes. It had to happen, and the trumpet resounded, and yet I didn't believe in these monstrosities, that now run inside me as in a hive. Cruel is the carousel that throws me from the landscape.

TOITS SOUS LA NEIGE

It was an entirely different city, which quickly rolled over on its other side, like it was turning in its sleep - quite far from winter's festive rooftops. Still, it is precisely this card, which he examines again and again, helping him remember those warm December evenings. The black branches march along the attic windows, and it only seems that the chimneys have found peace – everything is painted with ashes. Still, it is precisely this card from the museum shop, this one here, which later they held up in the red light of a sign, as if hoping to summon snow, that makes him knock against his memories like an insect against glass.

A COMMENT FOR YOUR INSOMNIA

Only a precise metaphor will defeat the hours of hate and thunder, when the wind drags away its nets, full of the remnants of our defeat, and when the crease of the sheet – *oh, how sad* – opens a casket to your dust-covered lips. The heart swiftly kicks out the heart of another.

SMOKE CISTERNS

A hydra of exhaust pipes billow out gray, choking clouds, in the puffs of which a blizzard swells - that veil for the houses' inflamed eyes, which look back at me, as I lose course, searching for the address. The lightbulb is too weak, like a mysterious fish swimming in the corridor's depths and illuminating numbers above the door. In a bar a young man sits next to me, in whose hand a petard once burst, and which is why indoors – in the smoke cisterns – he is wearing a black glove. Missing a thumb, it reminds one of a small rake, which scoops up money from a sticky counter. Oh, the season of ashes and boredom!

TRANSFORMATIONS

It is emptiness between radio stations, it is a demanding sign of "we," dissolving in the static, which forces you to scream. He turns you like a clock, he imprisons you in stillness like a flaming leaf. Meanwhile waves break in the sea, full of promises – and perhaps that's why you resemble a blossom, turning away from its own reflection.

THE DARKNESS WAS A CYLINDER

After roaming through muddy courtyards beset by worn-out cats, while a fire burns inside an old sidecar as the symbol of all ugliness, we climbed the tower and looked over the city's hunched back, where the factory chimneys formed brushstrokes of sleepy smoke. "There, where the rooftops are folded in stanzas like poetry," I remembered the words of hell's cook, there the glimmering station lifted its head – an iron-ribbed cupola. The darkness was a cylinder, brought by flocks of pigeons. Your blouse rippled airily like a ghost stuck in branches as you kissed my frozen ears. I stood deaf, and the sounds, which approached, were merely short shadows.

IN A PORT TOWN

The anchor is raised, every day it is heavier, and the night ship continues on its way, passing through granite squares. In the park birds flutter – old, crumpled newspapers, until they get stuck in the branches with a quiet tear. The cobblestones live like strangers beneath cargo trucks, which, as the coal dust blows about, search for the harbor; but occasionally the side street thunders in memory of the black horses and white linen in top boots. In a room gnats swarm above a breast carefully undressed, like an envelope cut with a knife. The bulb is dimmed, and in the window's arc a bird waves, as the lovers leave the granite coast.

TRAVELING SALESMAN

In Brussels I finally understood – my life is a patchwork constellation, barely held together by a few dull hopes. The suitcase became heavier with each step, as if time was stuffing rocks in it; in a suburban park kids shot blueberries at me – my company shirt, it seemed, had come down with chicken pox. In the church towers my clients' doors slammed ever louder. In the night, having missed the last train to Ghent, I wandered aimlessly through the station's digestive system until I collapsed at a hotdog stand, and in my hands, like an unstable apparition, a train schedule twinkled.

THE SEVENTH ZONE
for Aivars

Trees on the hills, lined around the city's ruins, cocking their arms back for the storm. The air is free like a trumpet before music; the futile work of the wasps and bumblebees slumbers in the ashy anther. As soon as somebody lay on the chippings and shavings, which have covered the sullen brick walls of the manor, he would hear the most beautiful roar of a chainsaw; however, for now it's just a hornets' nest mutely announcing a twilight procession through homes and gardens, wide open and pillaged like the thoraxes of the dead. Look, an abandoned barn, the plume of which is plucked by the wind. Humiliated, it awaits the moment when it can collapse entirely. Fleshy maggots dissolve in glass wool and a serpent approaches his prey – slowly, as a bride to the altar. What an absent stare by the sooty stained glass windows … in God's image the trashcans burn.

NARCISSUS

Each mirror – a sunflower, turned towards his paws, even lakes, among which he'll disappear in the morning, shake like curtains in a foggy frame. Because his eyes follow his caresses like a dervish does the wispy smoke. Because he knows – fingers beat their victim like a drum. Just like at dawn he'll realize it only takes a night for a hammock to become a straitjacket.

MARTYR

"That intoxication from the puffs of your breath, where as among the clouds, it seems, wine valleys appear for a moment," he will justify himself at last, bent over the table, "it forces me to compare a vase to a mouth, and sandbanks – breasts uncovered by a sheet. That luxury, when everything is something else. And, if it isn't something else, then at the very least it's vague, overshadowed, waning, seen at an angle or crossed by a jealous surface – a smile through milk glass or a sore under a gauze."

I will pull him through things, parting them like waves, even though he wanted to kiss me the way a magnet kisses a magnet.

THE MORNING BEFORE THE REVOLUTION

The queen's head, shrouded with rumor and piercing glances, is lifted from the birds' feathers – there is not a sentence deeper than a child's shoe, just slight resemblances, dangerously approaching sadness. Just the snow-white bonnet of the servant floats in the morning light. "Just the sun's merciless gong, against which, arriving from the west, thunder's clubs strike." Laying under the canopy they bolt upright, the lovers irked, they seem like toys, which must live with springs in their backs.

THE ARENA

Like a toreador with a bull in red sand, imprisoned behind the rattling bars – will we be freed by sweet barbarities which squander bodies in a shadow theater and draw the arena's horizon closer? Until the thick hair becomes dust-stuffed blossoms, but the muscles' silt – there the arms must be lodged in death. Until the curses grow thorns in loamy curls and in the eyes' brownness, terror floods in, striking from the depths of one's forehead. Was I the first whose caress was covered by a glove?

THE SLEEPWALKERS

And it rises up, as if swaying from drunkenness, merely a corner of a whole – a defunct fountain, the reserved crown of a poster pillar and other flowers. Further on buildings amass in the fog, canals flow like scarfs from the sleeve of the night, and waves gallop on the dark backs of fish. Once again the hour is nigh, smitten by its thorn – *how beautiful a wound is* – and the empty park, where we once by chance went down to the water, frightening the rats, and the light covered us like a torn-up cloth. If you find me lying there right in the middle, place the key in my hunched back – you're the only one – and turn it quickly.

POST-FACTUM

Look, our loving remains have been unearthed: a finger secured in a finger just for the sake of a beautiful image, the mute floodgates of a hair clip next to cheeks adorned with little legs that have fallen off – a proud entourage of decay, though it's just a reflection of lost splendor, and in the mirror's half-moon our intolerable features disappear like a malicious joke, for the briefest moment was trampled, while the beak of forgiveness – from inside, like a key in a dark room – pecked at our breast.

VOICES BETWEEN THE SCREAMS

They believed in ___, but time___ or water covers one's hand, then colors ___ and muddles ___, although it was fine to begin with, ___ in anger they mocked everyone, who ___, fall's torn paths ___ like rain unfurls on one's shoulders, while the eyes ___ hands tried to catch the reddest one from ___, in the bag there's a photo and scissors, ___ to allot to another, however at times it still seemed ___, if only quieter ___ in a place without its own face ___, look, the clouds have opened up, ___, until they disintegrate like ___.

HANZA STREET

Standing on the balcony at night – to the left the moon ducks between the chimneys, to the right a couple disappears through Alexander's Gate – and out of lonely pretense you roll the cork of a carafe made of clear Bohemian glass between your fingers. Standing like a landowner in his dressing gown with a landscape before him and not realizing that this moment, seemingly *yours* alone, belongs to an entirely different life, which unexpectedly has curled like a ribbon picked up by a gust of wind, so that a moment later it can return to the darkness. What shards does this perfect sphere hold within itself?

AFTER STĒRSTE
Jelgava, end of the 19th century

The fine snow breaks up easily and the street sweepers gather it in tubs, drag it down narrow streets, away from the market square, where, covered with blue nets, frozen horses fidget. The gaslight shines in the half-blind mirror of the shop: its slow rays write with golden letters. The twilight looks into the eyes of little porcelain beasts. Tinsel falls upon the forehead of a new century, while on the Christmas tree glass baubles with cheerful fairy-tale characters rock as if under a spell. It smells of wax; almonds, and raisins are being served on the table, while glasses are filled with currant wine. The city's roofs weave a gray shawl and tuck in the old world, a world whose heartbeats are not shots in silence, whose snow is not yet ashes. Like heavy-hearted clouds they will slide among those who will survive, among the houses' naked chimneys.

LETTERS TO SUSETTE

A northeasterly blows, Hölderlin's favorite wind, since 1803 at least, when he composed the hymn "Andenken" in Tübingen, and until this very moment under totally different poplars. They could be buds in a gradual explosion or September shadows, filled with blossoms (if you have to wander in time), but I fail to vanish there with you who forever remains in a foreign land. That's how Hölderlin lived, thinks Susette, the wife of a Frankfurt banker – Diotima in later texts – to whom he wrote regularly, until he lost his mind and Zimmer the carpenter, an educated man, gave him a room in a tower with a view to the river and meadows. No trace of brown-tanned flesh exists anymore, just an eclipse of images.

LYING ON ONE'S SIDE DURING A FEVER

The small, royal radio – whose sloping silver scepter picks up slow and summer-like music, just as irritating as grasshoppers' dry wings – hides a lightning-shaped crack in the wall, a shallow and dusty split, which you can't tear wider, as you can, for example, cheap fabric. And that is why there is only this room with the small, royal radio, against the grill of which dry wings crash like a phantom memory of the lazy blows of a scythe in an overgrown field. And they echo in one another until I once again fall asleep and dream about a new togetherness. A mountain of autumnal creepers, where happy people come to drink above the city's jittery lights.

A CLASSIC

Oh, rose-colored hillside! Innocent smoke curls around the cathedral, along the stream and ruins of apples, down below a train darts by, in which I fail to wake up and I swing like an empty sleeve. Oh, greedy hills, to which each tiny blossom surrenders itself! Oh, twilight, when the harvester's cart conducts mass with a whip! Each time that I succeed in opening my eyes, I am like a child put in front of a fun-house mirror for the first time. Though it's not a mirror, but a landscape with a cloud, in whose lampshade a cross lights up, and my fall knows no end.

WINDOWS OVERLOOKING THE JANÁČEK EMBANKMENT

Prague before Christmas. An enthusiastic guide, dressed like an angel, shows the brightly-lit facades of the buildings, nude gods and armored saints. Tourists whisper underneath tattered wings. I find refuge in an alleyway with a snow-covered catafalque and a church's stained glass window. The Star of Bethlehem swings between red and blue; faith loses any seriousness it had. In Janáček's riverfront windows a family gathers under a chandelier ... all that's missing is soft music, as I stand on the sidewalk below, blinded by the snowstorm. And even on the night tram, which takes me, slightly tipsy, back up the hill, there's no place for unhindered sadness. Because in the depths of the car someone is peeling a tangerine.

BRATISLAVA

We walked through the rain thinking about Weiner-Kráľs painting "Básnik" in which one can see, behind the corner of a dilapidated house, a figure flying away in the night: the black edges of a vagabond's hat and the gray locks framing an unnaturally large eye, the pant legs – one with a red patch on it – that are empty, frozen in a barely-visible ripple, and a pale hand, which still hopes to throw the last violet onto the sidewalk. We thought about a poet, who is blown away by the indifferent winds of history, as easily as paper. In a bar near the Mladost cinema we drank beer and talked about Europe, which at that time was tumbling slowly but surely like the Tower of Pisa. The wise Indian looked into my eyes and expressed his condolences for times that I would go through, while a plump Slovak waitress lit a tealight under the Dubliner's wrinkled forehead, and I reminded them of *tikkun olam* as a promise hidden in today's ruins. It was a few months before the catastrophe – an evening in a half-empty city, as three figures blurred by the rain wait for a tram, measuring the pulse of a continent according to the silence on the streets.

SERMON

The window of our room swings fragilely on a hinge resembling a partially torn-off ear for the November winds to scoff at. Meanwhile the others gather in a torch-lit procession and a bronze figure honors them, by taking off his hat, while we, breathing in our hands, await the rat's sermon. And then the scratches preach: "Whatever comes to pass, let us be brothers in oatmeal and cheese."

VALDEMĀRS STREET

The thunder of dark motors startles the treetops, windowpanes light up in anger, and the rain washes our faces away – stains on glass. Fear increases in strength – like the wind, which breaks loose from the labyrinth of streets, so it can choke your neck. The quiet song of bones: "Remember me, remember me." Youth in long hallways, where clocks continue their dance of death, in our alien apartment, where we burst out in nervous laughter.

This stubbornness with which we left·one another.

THREE PHOTOGRAPHS

FOR MY PARENTS

A gaze, as it is known, is the simplest of gestures. Surfacing from the depths of silence – from a word, which sprouts inside itself like a solitary plant – it strives to illuminate its origin, which it abandoned, as a lamp might abandon a ceiling vault as it's dimming. Such is also the gaze of Franz's boyhood, and, if the greenhouse with palm branches, unacquainted with southerly winds, is inclined to disappear, then the eyes will look past us for a long time still. The boy's little lace-adorned suit jacket, it seems, is somewhat tight for him, the Spanish hat a discus for his fine fingers, and you can never know the moment the clumsily-grasped stick is charming. But the left ear – an attentive gramophone blossom, which is only able to listen – searches for sounds of the future, and perhaps that is the mouse's song from a damp and unfinished world.

However, there is yet another gaze – having lifted the boy carefully – as if with tweezers – into an unfamiliar landscape, where heavenly sighs still murmur in the dry leaves of the palms. When he moved once again,

as if he was a branch himself, when he returned to his own body as if coming from a distant island, did the applause thunder like a motor's pistons? Franz performed on the dark stage of memory, but not for himself – shackled in his jacket like a magician's box, which is sawed in half, the feeble bourgeois stood as a sign for a happy life but one that was designed for another. And a dusty cough forced its way from his breast.

But, if he were to perform in the Orel apartment theatre – the hat made Asja's face more beautiful, just as an array of stars knows how to adorn a remote hill – would his sorrows then vanish among the orphans, who run around like dogs or vigorously flail their arms about, emulating the storm-harried trees? And how would he carry on, if a group of dirty little thieves barged into the studio, armed with knobsticks, with the leader shoving him with his boot as he enters the circle of nature? Perhaps Franz would step aside: like a crab he would crawl closer to a damp corner, running from a gesture to a gesture. It's only those with paper hats that still have hope.

*

Walter's turbid, resolute gaze looks out over the landscape, which he had conquered, having climbed up the hill, while his little brother's face exudes a strange peace – it seems he is looking at the dust from the wheels of childhood and at the same time is letting himself be overshadowed by a ruminative triumph, the hour of which strikes like in a clock, which is turned ahead – suddenly they are grown. Especially Walter's seriousness – it is far from the carefree butterfly hunts in Berlin's suburbs where – with the garden path snaking into bushes and undergrowth – he himself became a butterfly, so he could catch in his net his own elective affinities, those submerged in the flowers' spells. Perhaps it is there in the leaves' rustling that he heard (for the first time) nature's laments and carried them over to his terse movements, as a Vanessa atalanta slowly approached – it didn't touch the plants either, but, suddenly, as if heeding some command, it flew to another blossom.

In Berlin he found shelter in the Kaiserpanorama's flanks – a cylinder-shaped monster, which serenely whirrs in the twilit room sectioned off by a heavy curtain. In place of a mouth there was a plaque with gleaming numbers, but the forehead was a peephole for names of far-flung places. Looking through one of the twenty five pairs of eyes, Walter observed the German landscapes: how sails bend under the terrifying clouds of Frisia or how the Schwarzwald mountains loom in the mist among the trunks. However, he was fascinated much more by the sudden, tropical light – born in the palms' lower branches, then rising a moment after the bell, which simultaneously, cheerily, and sorrowfully announces a change of image, it followed the boy home. So it could fall like a veil upon the darkness of the desk.

When, with the imagination waning, the burner door lost the sailing ship's story and the room's palm tree didn't invite one to drop anchor at the edge of the alcove balustrade, led by a strange anxiety, he wrapped himself in a curtain like a magic cloak – the specter of the decline of Biedermeier, lending his body to the premises until the moment he became startled by a telephone call coming from the corridor's valley. Pressing his head between the vulcanite receivers, which were like two disfigured hands, cool and heavy like dumbbells, Walter surrendered to his friend's enthusiastic speech, which was occasionally pierced through in a line by intrusions, similar to a mouse's squeaking, which exists only among those boys' voices. Afterwards he returned to the window. Below, on the street, a lantern is lit above a horse's ornamented neck, and a dim light exposes the gloomy brick walls of evening.

*

The daguerreotype's pioneers foresaw that the little faces trapped in photos were watching, so clear is their gaze that it fills an observer with a fear of looking back. And if, in this image, held now between my fingers, there would be something from the photograph's childhood, if I managed to believe in such miracles – as Walter tried to believe in the sounds of the church bell in the depths of the panorama – would I discover some uninterrupted "I" that would speak to me like a close friend, or should everything be left scattered like that string of islands in a recent dream? Cheap clothes, a small warped bench on a crumbling background – it all seems so foreign, just like that boy's gaze, which I can't understand, and which burrows into me without longing, stumbling across the emptiness of non-memory.

My childhood lacked – and still lacks – deciphering, because what did that monkey's gesture (both mystical and simple) really mean? Did it unite me with the world of my ancestors, which is possible solely as a sketch between sleep and wakefulness? Perhaps in that child there's a sort of anxious trepidation that still remains – is that why I covered the beast with my arm so fearlessly? Now, having returned to my summer house, I can push the low attic door open and imagine. It opens also to the boy, who I was once. We both take a step on cold embers inhabited by forgotten things. I will also lose my color in the same way, and perhaps the vague hint of some image will manage to stir my memory – that fanciful flower, which is a stage for my shadow.

NOTES

"After Rilke" (p. 19) is a reference to Rainer Maria Rilke's poem "Archaic Torso of Apollo," in particular the first paragraph and beginning of the second (translated by Stephen Mitchell):

> We cannot know his legendary head
> with eyes like ripening fruit. And yet his torso
> is still suffused with brilliance from inside,
> like a lamp, in which his gaze, now turned to low,
> gleams in all its power.

The image of the raven in "After Rike" comes from Greek mythology. Ravens were associated with Apollo, the god of prophecy, and seen as god's messengers in the mortal world.

"Touts sous la neige" (p. 22) is a reference to French Impressionist Gustave Caillebotte's painting "Rooftops in the Snow," which was completed in 1879 and hangs in the Musée d'Orsay.

"There, where the rooftops are folded in stanzas like poetry" (p. 26) is a line from a poem by the Latvian poet Linards Tauns (1922-1963). Tauns came to New York City in 1950 where he established a collective of young Latvian modernist poets called the Hell's Kitchen Group.

"The Seventh Zone" (p. 29) is a reference to Latvian poet Aivars Madris's six-part poetry cycle "Zones Without People" (2015).

"After Stērste" (p. 38) uses childhood memories written by Latvian poet Elza Stērste (1885-1976).

"Bratislava" (pp. 43–44) – *tikkun olam* is a concept in Judaism (literally "the repair of the world") marking the abolition of injustice created by history that will come with the beginning of the Messianic Era.

In "Three Photographs" (pp. 49-59), Franz is a reference to the German-speaking Bohemian Jewish writer Franz Kafka (1883-1924); Asja is the nickname of Latvian actress and theater director Anna Lācis (1891-1970), who was the lover of Walter Benjamin; Walter refers to German Jewish philosopher Walter Benjamin (1892-1940).

During World War I, Anna Lācis lived in the Russian city of Orel, where she organized an improvisational theater for children. During their acting exercises, the children embodied the roles of different animals, however the street children were best at roles as criminal types. Franz took part in Asja's theater group – the main impulse for this historically impossible scene is the description of the Nature Theatre of Oklahoma (essentially a theater of gestures) found in Kafka's novel *Amerika*:

> "We are a theater that can make use of everyone, each in his place!"

In addition, individual motifs from Kafka's works used in the poem can be found in Benjamin's 1934 essay "Franz Kafka: On the Tenth Anniversary of His Death" from the collection of essays and reflections entitled "Illuminations." The ideas for the poetic photographic interpretations were provided by Benjamins's essay entitled "A Short History of Photography" (1931), whereas the facts and associations about Benjamin's childhood came from his 1930 short prose collection "Berlin Childhood around 1900."